Where t NORTH WEST ENGLAND

AN INFORMATIVE GUIDE TO EATING OUT IN THE NORTH WEST

Editor: Alison Moore
Art and Design: Simon Baker, Michelle Power
Editorial Assistant: Rebecca Norris
Compilation: Len Rainford

CONTENTS

Cover Photograph: Yang Sing Restaurant, Manchester
Tastes of North West England by Sue Morgan

Published by Kingsclere Publications Ltd.
Highfield House, 2 Highfield Avenue,
Newbury, Berkshire, RG14 5DS

Produced by the Norman W. Hardy Printing Group, 112 Bermondsey Street, London SE1 3TX.
Tel: 01 378 1579 at Avon Litho Ltd.

Extreme care is taken to ensure the accuracy of entries, but
neither the Editor nor the Publishers accept any liability
for errors, omissions or other mistakes, or any
consequences arising therefrom.
All prices are correct at time of going to press.

1

Foreword

Keith and Nerys Mooney

by Keith Mooney

W hen my wife Nerys and I came to La Belle Epoque as restaurateurs over 15 years ago, there were four places to eat in Knutsford. Today there are over 35, including Italian, German, Indian and French cuisine, from simple pub grub to international haute cuisine.

This gives some idea of the public's awareness and knowledge of food and wine. This growth has been reflected throughout the North West which, as an area, can boast as many restaurants as anywhere in Britain, with the possible exception of London.

Our own restaurant, housed in an Italianate building built by an eccentric Englishman and serving French cuisine, typifies the diversity of the area.

But there are so many more restaurants waiting to be discovered, and the area is blessed by considerable natural beauty, from the Pendle and Ribble valleys to the quiet, leafy lanes of Cheshire.

I do hope that *Where to Eat in North West England* will help you discover many gastronomic delights that make dining out one of life's greatest pleasures.

Keith Mooney
Proprietor, La Belle Epoque, Knutsford

 Preface

E ngland's North West is a region of surprising contrasts, containing many of Britain's best loved and most famous holiday resorts, such as Blackpool, Morcambe, Southport and Lytham St. Annes, as well as its famous cities of Manchester, Liverpool and historic Lancaster and Chester.

The North West has a bit of everything, all readily accessible by it's superb motorway network. The great variety of tourist and leisure opportunities is attracting more visitors than ever before, and consequently the need for good eating places is increasing.

Dining out in the North West can be as varied as the tourist attractions. The major cities abound with fine restaurants and café bars, catering for all tastes and nationalities. Award winning museums and heritage centres provide many excellent and interesting watering holes, the historic towns have numerous quaint coffee shops whilst the beautiful Ribble Valley, the Peak District, the Pennine Moors and rural Cheshire boast some of the most delightful country pubs and restaurants in the country.

Some years ago, the North West Tourist Board adopted the slogan 'surprisingly different', which applies equally to both its tourist attractions and to its culinary skills. Regional dishes which flourish here are very much a part of the North West experience, and dining out really is 'surprisingly different'.

I hope that this excellent guide helps you discover the delights of eating out in the North West — you may be surprised but you won't be disappointed.

For further information, contact Ron Graham (Marketing Manager), North West Tourist Board.

Tastes of NORTH WEST ENGLAND

For centuries the housewives of North West England fulfilled their household duties, — cooking the daily meals; making jams, preserves and pickles in season; tending a vegetable plot; nurturing the household's livestock — and, in spare moments(!), spinning wool into yarn which would be either woven into cloth by the men of the house or traded with itinerant chapmen. Then the Industrial Revolution brought the invention of machines which drew spinners and weavers away from their rural homes to the mills in the burgeoning towns. Long working hours in the mills absorbed most of the time and energy of the women and threatened the traditional skills of the housewife. Fortunately traditional cuisine survived in rural areas and improvements in conditions of employment and prosperity eventually freed women sufficiently to engage in household pursuits again.

Breakfasts were, when time and resources allowed, substantial, and a cooked breakfast, served with oatcakes, would include Lancashire's own Black Pudding. A steaming bowl of porridge was a popular rib-lining start to the day, most relished when a spoonful of treacle, imported from the West Indies through Liverpool, was poured over the top. Mid-day meals, secure from dirt or damage in 'snap' tins, were handed to the men as they set off to work in the foundries and collieries. Sustaining savoury pasties, Lancashire Foots — so named because the shape of the pastry was reminiscent of the sole of a foot — were sturdy fillers for snap tins and hungry men. Lancashire Hot Pot became a particular favourite during the 19th Century, partly because women working in the mills could set a pot filled with neck of mutton or lamb, onions and carrots, topped with a layer of potatoes, on the fire before they went to work in the morning, to be greeted on their return in the evening by not only a delectable aroma but also a meal ready to serve to the family.

Other dishes, such as Lobscouse — a stew of beef or mutton and root vegetables — from Liverpool, and steamed steak and kidney puddings — perhaps enriched with a few oysters — which required long, slow cooking, featured regularly in homes where mothers went out to work. Chester's Hot Pork Pie — pork chops in a rich

gravy, enhanced with apples and onions and covered with a crisp short pastry crust — was another popular main meal, even though it demanded a little more attention than a Hot Pot or Stew.

In rural areas the customary household pig was kept with typical Northern efficiency. Fattened on kitchen scraps and whey (a by-product of cheese making) the pig was the basis of recipes and dishes which made use of every part except the squeak. Black pudding, chitterlings, pork loaf,

bacon, polony, sausages and pork pies are but a few of the pork products which can be found in butchers' shops and on the table as a savoury course of a traditional high tea. Ham, or bacon, and eggs would precede a generous spread including bread and butter, a selection of 'cut-and-come-again' cakes and cold puddings, such as jelly or trifle, all washed down with copious cups of tea. This type of evening meal was enjoyed by members of all levels of society, although in poorer homes on weekdays the spread might not have ranged far beyond chitterlings or tripe and onions followed by bread and jam.

During the summer the hot dish at high tea would be substituted for salad with ham, potted meat or potted Morecambe Bay shrimps.

Fleetwood, a major fishing port, lands, amongst other sea foods, cod and plaice, much of which is crisp fried in batter and served with chips. Although hot, strong tea remains the staple beverage of the North, beer provides cool refreshment. The major national brewers are well represented but some 'real ales' can be found in the region. Moorehouses of Burnley brew real ales, including Pendle Witches Brew, which is available in a number of pubs and hotels including the Royal Hotel in Cleveleys, near Blackpool

In early times a watch or 'Wake' would be kept during the night preceding a religious festival. The term 'Wake' survives to this day, and many traditional foods are now served as part of Wakes celebrations. *Hen de la Wakes* which has corrupted to 'Hindle Wakes' is a hen, stuffed with prunes, simmered until cooked the day before a fair or festival, then served cold with lemon sauce at the main meal during the Wake day. Eccles cakes, traditionally associated with Eccles Wake — four days of fun and feasting in August — are to be found the year through these days, and are usually made with flaky pastry, although originally the pastry was short crust. Bury simnel cake, decorated with marzipan flowers and almond paste balls representing the eleven disciples (Judas is not included), is made and eaten in celebration of Mothering Sunday.

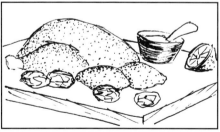

Dairy cows seen in the Goosnargh area are likely to be producing milk for the excellent traditional Lancashire cheeses made on nearby farms.

Cheshire cheese, which is mentioned in the *Domesday Book* has always been made from cows milk, unlike many other English cheeses the origins of which lie in goats' or ewes' milk. The tradition of cheesemaking is still strongly upheld in Cheshire's dairying area, particularly in the Malpas, Nantwich and Chester localities, where a number of cheesemakers are producing tangy farmhouse Cheshire cheeses.

The increasing popularity of international cuisine leads today's diner to hotels, restaurants and inns which offer dishes originating in England, the Middle East, Japan and places in between and beyond, as the pages of this guide will show. However, despite strong pressure from outside influences, the traditional cuisine of the region endures and is still to be found, so that eating out in the region can offer an opportunity for you to experience for yourself the *Tastes of North West England*.

Chef's Choice

In each of our regional **Where to Eat** guides, we ask an experienced chef, well-respected in the area, to provide one of his favourite menus:

Gary Jenkins

After a move to Oxfordshire to widen his experience, he came to The Three Gates where he has developed a style of modern British cuisine using only fresh ingredients and local produce.

STARTER
Hot Cheese Soufflé served with a Panache of Autumn Vegetables
This starter takes a little longer than most, using local cheeses to make the light, savoury soufflé accompanied by warm, baby vegetables and honey relish. Ideal for the Autumn and very popular at The Three Gates.

WINE
Savigny — Lès-Beaune 1985
A delicate, fruity red burgundy from a small vineyard just outside the town of Beaune.

Gary Jenkins is the head chef at The Three Gates Restaurant in Woodford, Cheshire. Following his basic training at Rochdale Festival College, Gary worked his formative years at Gleneagles and quality restaurants in Cheshire, gaining his first head chef position, at the age of 24, at The Georgian House Restaurant.

FISH COURSE
Steamed Fillet of Monkfish wrapped in Garden Leaves, surrounded by a Basil Scented Sabayon.
This dish can be used as a first or main course. Monkfish has become a very popular fish in the last few years. Not one of the best looking fish around, but, once prepared and cooked properly it is very enjoyable.

WINE
Alsace Gerwürztraminer
The wine is excellent with fish and one of my favourites.

DESSERT
White Chocolate and Strawberry Terrine
A delicate, white chocolate mousse layered with freshly picked strawberries, set aside a pool of raspberry sauce and garnished with fresh strawberries and raspberries, dusted with a touch of icing sugar and topped with a sprig of mint.

WINE
Crémant de Loire 1976
This is a good quality sparkling wine from Anjou and Touraine, an excellent complement to a sweet course.

MAIN COURSE
Rack of Cheshire Lamb cooked in a Sweet Cider Sauce with Forest Mushrooms and Bramley Apple Dumplings
This dish uses only the finest Cheshire Lamb, cooked pink with the simplest of ingredients. I designed this dish with subtle flavours to mix well together and look very effective on the plate.

WINE
Château Ramage-la-Batisse Cru Bourgeois Haut Médoc 1983
The wine is an outstanding Bordeaux wine, a perfect accompanyment to the lamb, and is found in the south west region of France at St Sauveur.

The meal should be finished with a good quality ground coffee and, at The Three Gates, we serve a selection of home-made liqueur chocolates, truffles and fudges.

Introduction

T his *Where to Eat* guide has been compiled to offer readers a good cross-section of eating places in the area. We do not only concentrate on the most expensive or the 'most highly rated' but endeavour to provide details of establishments which cater for all tastes, styles, budgets and occasions. Readers may discover restaurants (formal and informal), pubs, wine bars, coffee shops and tearooms and we thank proprietors and managers for providing the factual information.

We do not intend to compete with the established 'gourmet guides'. *Where to Eat* gives the facts — opening hours and average prices — combined with a brief description of the establishment. We do not use symbols or ratings. *Where to Eat* simply sets the scene and allows you to make the choice.

We state whether an establishment is open for lunch or dinner and prices quoted are for an à la carte three course meal or a table d'hôte menue, including service, as well as an indication of the lowest priced wine. However, whilst we believe these details are correct, it is suggested that readers check, when making a reservation, that prices and other facts quoted meet their requirements.

Two indexes are included at the back of the guide so that readers can easily pinpoint an establishment or a town or village. We always advise readers to use these indexes as, occasionally, late changes can result in establishments not appearing in a strictly logical sequence.

We hope that *Where to Eat* will provide you with the basis for many intimate dinners, special family occasions, successful business lunches or, perhaps, just an informal snack. A mention of this guide when you book may prove worthwhile. Let us know how things turned out. We are always pleased to hear from readers, be it praise, recommendations or criticism. Mark you envelopes for the attention of 'The Editor, Where to Eat Series'. Our address is:

Kingsclere Publications Ltd.
Highfield House, 2 Highfield Avenue,
Newbury, Berkshire, RG14 5DS.

We look forward to hearing from you. Don't forget, *Where to Eat* guides are now available for nearly every region of Britain, Ireland and the Channel Islands, each freshly researched and revised every year. If you're planning a holiday contact us for the relevant guide. Details are to be found within this book.

Where to Eat
NORTH WEST ENGLAND

YANG SING RESTAURANT

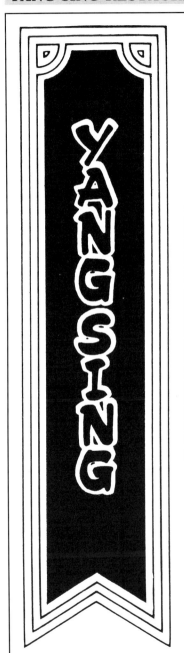

YANG SING RESTAURANT

34 PRINCESS STREET, MANCHESTER M14 JY
Tel: 061·236·2200

YANG SING RESTAURANT

Princess Street, Manchester. Tel: (061) 236 2200.

Hours: *Open for dinner midday – 11pm.*

Average Prices: *Five course banquet £16.*

Wines: *House wine £5.95 per bottle.*

As well as re-establishing itself as an important business centre outside London, Manchester also boasts the largest Chinese community in the North West — vibrant, colourful and exciting, it is a whole country within a city. It is also THE place to eat, and situated on its edge in a splendid Victorian building is the internationally renowned Yang Sing Restaurant. A visit to this highly popular Cantonese eating-house is an experience in itself, its noise and bustle, and darting waiters a visible adjunct to the sizzling heat of the huge busy kitchen. The speciality is mainly Cantonese food, and with a menu of over 250 dishes, considerable culinary artistry and a large kitchen staff is needed to ensure its smooth preparation. The result is an opportunity to taste a wide variety of Chinese food, particularly the delicate Chinese appetiser Dim Sum, prawns and scallops lent new flavour by skilful chefs, steamed spare ribs, crispy duck, inspiring soups, whilst the adventurous can try beancurd and tripe dishes with squid and sea slug...the list is endless and irresistible! As well as catering to the general public in its 140 seat restaurant, the Yang Sing also boasts private banqueting rooms with a capacity of over 300, providing dinner tailored to meet the requirements of the most well-travelled of businessmen. Yet, whether it be for one or 100 guests, service is always friendly and courteous. Not surprisingly with such a popular restaurant, booking well in advance is advisable, with often as long as four weeks for Fridays and Saturdays, but with its vast cuisine, extensive catering facilities, and the lively aura of a restaurant on the move, the wait is well worth it. Visa and Access are welcome.

BAVARDAGE PRIVATE MEMBERS CLUB

Manchester. Tel: (061) 8323117.
Hours: *Open for lunch Mon – Fri; dinner Wed – Sat.*
Average Prices: *A la Carte £15.*

Bavardage Private Members Club has boasted an elite and sophisticated clientele from Manchester's cafe society, including the internationally rich and famous, since its inception in 1982. Renowned for its relaxing ambience, Bavardage has created the convivial brasserie-style surroundings that provide the perfect backdrop for the discerning executive. From the sublime to the simple, the gourmet menu offers a mouthwatering selection of cosmopolitan cuisine to enhance the lunchtime business meeting or friendly get together. In the evening, while away your time into the mellow hours with excellent food, drink and a superb range of music — from jazz, rock and pop to classical. They cordially invite you to partake of their renowned hospitality, sample the cuisine and, most importantly, enjoy yourself. Carriages at 2am.

BAVARDAGE · 10 BACKBRIDGE ST · MANCHESTER · TEL: 061-832 3117

MARKET RESTAURANT

Edge Street, Manchester. Tel: (061) 834 3743.

Hours: *Open for dinner only Tues – Sat until 9.30pm. Closed Sun/ Mon.*

Average Prices: *A la Carte £14.*

Wines: *House wine £3.50 per bottle.*

A cream and green decor lends a 50's touch to this cosy city centre restaurant. Situated opposite the old Smithfield Markets, it has been transformed into one of Manchester's most popular restaurants, earning mentions in all the major food guides. Fresh seasonal produce, cooked with flair and attractively presented, is the hallmark of the Market. A monthly changing menu, with an emphasis on Modern British Cooking brings fish to the fore in dishes such as monkfish with ginger, and poached trout fillets or brill. Old favourite bread and butter pudding is a dessert suggestion, or perhaps an orange cardamom ice cream. Desserts are something of a speciality — their excellence has led to the formation of a monthly 'Pudding Club' (booking is essential), which is held in the newly opened Elizabeth Raffald room. A fine range of wines includes many 'New World' varieties, and Hugh Rock's elderflower and sparkling gooseberry. The atmosphere is enhanced by the marvellously eclectic choice of music. Vegetarians catered for, and credit cards welcome.

AA/Egon Ronay Recommended — Licensed

Edge Street / 104 High Street
Manchester M4 1HQ Tel: 061 834 3743
Open evenings Tuesday to Saturday from 5-30pm
Bookings Welcome

Close to the Craft Village — Free on-street Parking

ISOLA BELLA

Dolefield, Crown Square, Manchester 3. Tel: (061) 831 7099.

Hours: *Open for lunch and dinner (last orders 10pm). Closed Sun.*

This long-established Italian restaurant is renowned as being one of the finest Italian restaurants in the North West, a reputation built on professional service and superb presentation. Magnificent surroundings, authentic dishes and a warm welcome make it the ideal setting for an intimate dinner or business lunch. A comprehensive wine list.

RISTORANTE

DOLEFIELD, CROWN SQUARE, MANCHESTER 3
Tel: 061-831 7099

A long-established Italian restaurant which has built its reputation on professional expertise and superb presentation. Provides an extensive menu of authenitic dishes and comprehensive wine list.

VILLAGE RESTAURANT

Ramsbottom, Greater Manchester. Tel: (070 682) 5070.

Hours: *Open for dinner at 8.30pm.*

Average Prices: *A la Carte £19.50.*

A terraced cottage is home to this highly unusual but extremely pleasant little husband-and-wife run restaurant, where leisurely and wholesome dining is the order of the day. Much love and money is lavished on Ros Hunter's 6-course dinners, and the formula is a highly successful one. Quality ingredients are capably handled — recipes employ hormone-free meats, organically grown vegetables, unpasteurised cheeses and organic flour, resulting in praiseworthy dishes such as brill in meunière sauce, spiced fillet of beef, and mushroom soup flavoured with lemon and sherry. The six courses necessitate lengthy dining in traditional old England style. The cellar supports such leisurely dining — a long list includes old clarets, Rhônes, Australian Grange Hermitage, and Californian Cabernet Sauvignons, whilst Mr johnson also allows diners to buy many wines by the glass, thus creating their own order to match the dinner. Parties and children are catered for, and there is ample parking. Access and Visa.

HENRY'S CAFÉ BAR

Parsonage Gardens, Manchester. Tel: (061) 832 7935.

Hours: *Open for breakfast (8 – 10.30am); lunch (11.30am – 3pm) and dinner (6 – 10pm).*

Wines: *House wines from £5.90 per bottle.*

Henry's Café Bar, situated just off Deansgate behind Kendals, is full of city centre style and atmosphere. The fountain and pillars set the scene for a dining-out experience to savour. Food is served all day, starting with The Breakfast Club, offering everything from traditional English fare to European dishes including Danish pastries and chocolate croissants. The international flavour is continued on the evening menu, with blinis from Russia, Tennessee Mushrooms and dolmades (stuffed vine leaves), amongst many other dishes, to choose from. Cocktails are a speciality, including a Bees-Knees, Barracuda or a Zombie. Henry's also serve non-alcoholic 'mocktails', and if your favourite drink does not appear on the menu, they will be delighted to make it for you.

DUKES CELLAR RESTAURANT

*Worsley Old Hall, Old Hall Lane, Worsley, Manchester.
Tel: (061) 799 5644.*

Hours: *Lunch Mon – Fri (12 – 2pm). Dinner Mon – Sat from 7pm.*

Average Prices: *A la Carte £15. Evening Table d'Hôte £10.95. Business lunch £6.50 (2 courses); £8.50 (3 courses).*

Wines: *House wine £7.50 per litre.*

Discover a new experience which has the flavour of the finest traditions. The historic Dukes Cellar Restaurant at Worsley Old Hall combines the subtle atmosphere of the past with the best of today's cuisine. Enjoy this discreet and charming setting where superb food and fine wines are matched by an old-fashioned understanding of the service and style. Delicious starters include smoked Scotch salmon and asparagus tips baked in puff pastry and served with Hollandaise sauce, or button mushrooms and strips of ham cooked in a cream and white wine sauce with a hint of garlic. Follow this with carré of lamb cooked with rosemary and sliced at your table, served with garlic butter. You will feel a sense of history at The Dukes Cellar which was once owned by the Duke of Bridgewater who built the famous Bridgewater canal.

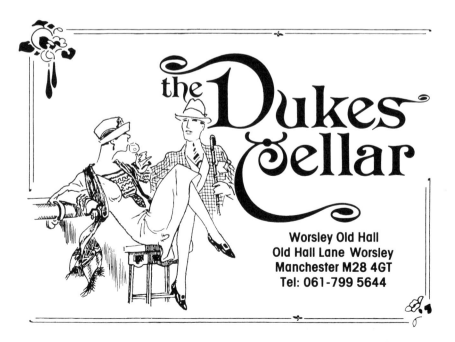

**Worsley Old Hall
Old Hall Lane Worsley
Manchester M28 4GT
Tel: 061-799 5644**

THE INN PLAICE FISH RESTAURANT

Whitworth Street, Manchester. Tel: (061) 236 5512.

Hours: *Open for lunch, dinner and bar meals until 11pm.*

Average Prices: *A la Carte £12; snacks from £1.50.*

Wines: *House wine £5.45 per bottle.*

The Inn Plaice must be one of THE in places to be in Manchester! Recently opened, it has been renovated on a large scale, and now specialises in fish dishes, catering practically 'from dawn 'til dusk'. Located just yards from the Palace Theatre, it has found a niche in the dining habits of both theatre-goers and the business world, and its popularity is ever increasing. Well spaced oak tables predominate, creating a welcoming restaurant and bar. Fish brought fresh from the Scottish fishing villages are transformed by chef George Smith into full flavoured, inventive dishes — starters of prawn cocktail, and avocado and prawns before a dish of lemon sole fillet, Scottish salmon, halibut, and lobster thermidor. There are also special dishes for children and vegetarians, and for everyone: George's 'pièce de resistance' — traditional freshly baked Lancashire pies. A fine choice of worldwide wines accompanies. All major cards.

48–50 WHITWORTH ST • MANCHESTER • 061-236 5512

PALMS GARDEN TERRACE

Royal Exchange Shopping Centre, Manchester.
Tel: (061) 834 9365.

Hours: *Open for coffee, tea and lunch until 5.30pm. Closed Sun.*
Average Prices: *A la Carte £9.*

Surrounded by a selection of stylish shops in this spacious arcade, the Palms Garden is the perfect balm for the weary shopper. Personal waitress service and a flexible cuisine are the hallmarks of this family run business, whose varied English menu offers anything from snacks to steaks, concluding with tempting speciality ice creams. There is a fully licensed bar.

SUPERB FOOD SERVED IN DELIGHTFUL SURROUNDINGS FULLY LICENSED BAR

ROYAL EXCHANGE SHOPPING CENTRE
(1ST FLOOR), CROSS ST, MANCHESTER. Tel. 061·834·9365

RAJDOOT TANDOORI

St. James House, South King Street, Manchester.
Tel: (061) 834 2176.

Hours: *Open for lunch and dinner (last orders 10.30pm).*
Average Prices: *A la Carte £15; Table d'Hôte £6.*

Recognised as being one of the best restaurants of its kind in the city, this long-established Indian restaurant has been recently refurbished in an authentic style. Service is friendly and efficient — manager Sant is well-known by customers who, over the last 17 years, have tended to become regulars.

Sant Mali welcomes you to Europe's most authentic Indian cuisine in elegant and exotic atmosphere

St. James House, South King Street   Tel: 061-834 2176/7092

ROYAL ORCHID AND SIAM ORCHID

36 Charlotte St. Manchester M14 FD: Tel 061·236·5183
54 Portland St. Manchester M1   : Tel 061·236·1388

Hours :   Open Mon – Fri 11.30 – 2.30, 6.30 – 11.30. Closed Sat lunch.
Siam closed Sun lunch. Royal Orchid closed Sun evening.
Royal open Sun lunch. Buffet 12 – 3.

THE LYMM HOTEL

Lymm, Cheshire. Tel: (0925) 752233.

Hours: *Open for coffee, lunch and dinner (last orders 10pm).*

Average Prices: *A la Carte £15; Sun lunch £8.*

Situated just outside the village of Lymm, this hotel is yet only minutes
from motorways, Manchester airport, and Warrington station. Recently
refurbished, it boasts 69 en suite bedrooms, and five fully equipped meeting
rooms. Relax in the appealingly decorated lounge bar, or dine on a
renowned English/French cuisine in the Bridgewater Restaurant. Live bands
and a pianist entertain. All major cards.

THE LORD DARESBURY HOTEL

Chester Road, Daresbury, Warrington, Cheshire WA4 4BB. Tel: (0925) 67331.

Hours: *Open for morning coffee, lunch, afternoon tea and dinner (last orders — 10pm).*

Average Prices: *Looking Glass Restaurant £13.95*
Terrace a La Carte £22.

Wines: *£8 per litre.*

Location, accessibility, luxury, comfort and a warm, friendly welcome are amongst some of the chracteristics that make the Lord Daresbury Hotel the ideal situation, whether it be for pleasure or business. Set in the heart of the Cheshire countryside, Alice in Wonderland provides the themes for the hotel with the books author, Lewis Carroll, having lived but a short walk away from the village of Daresbury. The Looking Glass Restaurant offers relaxed and friendly service, with a selection of traditional roasts from the carvery — Carroll's tables. Alternatively, should you wish to dine off the Daresbury Market menu, a table d'hôte menu with a selection of carefully chosen dishes for the more discerning palate, to which customers are readily enticed by the adventurous touches to the cuisine. The Terrace Restaurant specialises in delicious cuisine moderne, using only the freshest market produce cooked to order. An extensive wine list complements the menu.

THE LORD DARESBURY HOTEL

CHESTER RD., DARESBURY,
WARRINGTON, CHESHIRE
WA4 4BN   DE VERE 🦢 HOTELS

Tel (0925) 67331
Fax (0925) 601264

THE BIRCH AND BOTTLE

Higher Whitley, near Warrington, Cheshire.
Tel: (0925) 73225.

Hours: *Open for coffee, lunch and dinner until 9.30pm. Bar meals.*
Average Prices: *A la Carte from £14; Table d'Hôte £8.50.*
Wines: *House wine £5.50 per bottle.*

Built in 1721, the Birch and Bottle is a traditional country inn with white-washed walls, low beams and a distinct olde worlde feel. Log fires burn in winter, and old pictures, brasses and antiques adorn the walls. Since taking over the former coaching inn six years ago, Ian and Sheila Holt have earned an enviable reputation for their traditional pub meals, whilst the new Conservatory Restaurant guarantees more stylish dining, its unusual black, green and pink decor providing a contrast in surroundings as well as cuisine. Traditional English food is served cooked fresh to order, and may include salmon hollandaise, chicken Kiev or scampi Neuberg, and an extensive wine list accompanies. Alternatively, for the more 'ad hoc' diner, delicious bar food is available, and a chance to sample some real ales — cask bitter and Greemans Mild among others. To add to the charm, the inn also hosts special gourmet and theme nights (Italian and French evenings perhaps), which bring a touch of 'ooh la la' to the historic inn. Children are welcome, as is payment by credit card.

CONSERVATORY RESTAURANT
BIRCH & BOTTLE

"Ian, Sheila and their friendly staff are waiting to welcome you."
NORTHWICH ROAD, HIGHER WHITLEY, NR WARRINGTON, CHESHIRE. WA4 4PH. TEL: 0925 73225

PELICAN INN AND MOTEL

Altrincham, Cheshire. Tel: (061) 962 7414.

Hours: *Open for coffee, lunch and dinner until 10pm.*
Average Prices: *A la Carte £12; Sun lunch £8.*
Wines: *House wine £7.45 per litre.*

Renowned for its friendly atmosphere, the Pelican 'welcome' is popular with both visitors and locals alike, and its claim to cater for every need should not be dismissed lightly. Minutes from Granada Studios, national motorways and Manchester Airport for which they offer superb flyaway packages, it is a useful place for the traveller 'en route'. The Manager, Brian Belcher, and his staff extend a warm welcome, offering 50 bedrooms, all recently refurbished with a high standard of facilities which include trouser presses, drink facilities and hairdriers. The inn's forte is to be found in the 'Wickers' restaurant; furnished in wicker with pastel colours, plants and marble statues, it is a lovely venue for dining on the interesting variety of traditional British food cooked well with care using the finest fresh ingredients, yet anything can be prepared. 'Whatever the customer wants, we do it' comes the boast from the kitchen staff! The ground floor location of the 'Wickers' is an added boon for those with disabilities, whilst children and vegetarians are equally well catered for. A sandwich open buffet bar provides lighter alternatives. All credit cards accepted.

WICKERS OF
TIMPERLEY

AT THE
PELICAN INN & MOTEL

DE VERE HOTELS

MANCHESTER RD, ALTRINCHAM,
CHESHIRE, WA14 5NH

Tel: 061·962·7414
Telex 061·668·014

RAIMONDO'S

The Downs, Altrincham, Cheshire. Tel: (061) 928 0912.

Hours: *Open for lunch, dinner and bar meals until midnight. Closed Sun.*

Average Prices: *Very reasonable from £3.95.*

Wines: *House wine £6.90 per carafe.*

Specialising in Italian and French cuisine, Raimondo's is the oldest family run restaurant in Altrincham, having traded for 24 years. Recently, a lounge bar has been opened upstairs, which makes an ideal venue for that leisurely drink. Tastefully decorated with an open log fire, spiral staircase and Italian furniture (for that touch of authenticity), it also has the added attraction of extended bar hours — a place to relax with friends and colleagues both before and after sampling the cuisine. With a seating capacity of 120, it can also be used for conferences, or private parties, when its Italianate charm and meals can be fully experienced. All the food is freshly prepared by Raimondo and his family, and with set menus available on request, parties of up to 50 can be catered for. Dining is a serious business here — lunchtime sees a wide choice of bar snacks and cheeses on offer, and as well as the main restaurant, a take away service is available. Frequent entertainment evenings see the addition of live music, completing the charm of this centrally located eating house. All credit cards are accepted.

Raimondo Ristorante
Italiano & Pizzeria

6 The Downs, Altrincham, Cheshire   061·928·0912

THE GEORGE AND DRAGON HOTEL

Altrincham, Cheshire. Tel: (061) 928 9933.

Hours: *Open for lunch, dinner and snacks 7 – 9.45pm.*

Average Prices: *A la Carte £17; Table d'Hôte £11; bar meals from £2.*

Wines: *House wine £7.60 per bottle.*

Situated in the lovely old town of Altrincham, only minutes from Manchester airport and motorways, this popular restaurant has that much valued ability to offer something for everyone. Ideally placed to explore the delights of rural Cheshire and Granada Studios — Europe's first theme television leisure park — it also boasts a fine local reputation for lunchtime bar snacks, and value for money. A restaurant subtly decorated in relaxing pastel blues and greys offers an alternative English cuisine. Saturday night dinner dances at only £15 per person combine great food, great company and great fun, and, should it all prove too tempting, 47 well-appointed luxury bedrooms are available. Sunday lunch is family time — enjoying a traditional roast in a pleasant environment will help to keep the youngsters out of mischief. Owned by County Inns, the hotel specialises in weekend leisure breaks — fun for all within easy reach of the bustle and beauty of historic Chester.

GEORGE AND DRAGON HOTEL

This attractive restaurant has a wide and enviable reputation for its fine wines, classical cuisine and impeccable service.

MANCHESTER ROAD, ALTRINCHAM, CHESHIRE WA14 4PH
Telephone: 061-928 9933

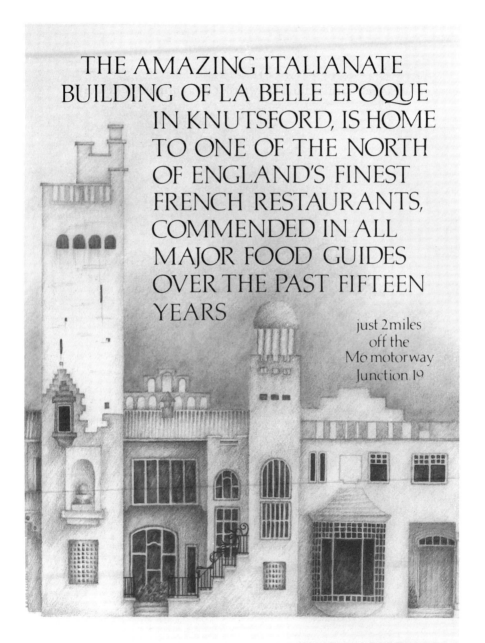

LA BELLE EPOQUE RESTAURANT

King Street, Knutsford. Tel: (0565) 3060.
Hours: *Open for dinner until 10pm. Closed Sun.*
Average Prices: *A la Carte from £21.*

One of Cheshire's architectural showpieces — a turn of the century Italianate building — makes a perfect setting for this French restaurant. Lovingly restored by the Mooney family over the past 15 years to recreate the Parisian Belle Epoque era, it boasts a dramatic art nouveau dining room which offers an exciting menu, the quality of which has been rewarded with recommendations in all major food guides. Chef David Williams makes skilful use of garden herbs and fresh local produce in both starters and main course. Lamb from Cheshire, duck from Lancashire, and blue cheese from Cashel make inventive dishes — breast of duck on apple purée, quail stuffed with nuts and nectarines, or calf's liver with cranberries and orange. One of Cheshire's most popular restaurants, its evocation of turn of the century Paris is so authentic that when the producers of 'Brideshead Revisited' shot their restaurant scenes here, not an item was changed. Parties are catered for, and credit cards will be accepted.

COTTONS HOTEL

Knutsford, Cheshire. Tel: (0565) 50333.
Hours: *Open for coffee, lunch and dinner until 10pm. Bar meals.*
Average Prices: *A la Carte £19; Table d'Hôte £12; snacks from £2.50.*
Wines: *House wine £7.95 per bottle.*

Welcome to the Cottons! Originally a 1920's roadside tea house owned by Mr and Mrs Cotton, this hotel now offers that age-old tradition of morning and afternoon tea in the Magnolia Lounge. The theme of French New Orleans brings high society colonial life into the heart of Cheshire — the accent is on style, comfort and good food; the result is a delightful, characterful hotel. The lavishly furnished Magnolia Restaurant seats 80, its ornate balconies making it an attractive eating venue. Cuisine is a combination of English, French and Creole, and its quality is one of the hotel's priorities. A wide choice may give you prawns, salmon, or perhaps a tropical fruit salad as starters to breast of chicken, steamed turbot or Scottish fillet. Several vegetarian dishes are available, and a taste from the specially selected French and German wines will complete the occasion. Sunday lunch at the Cottons is enlivened by a jazz band, whilst the hotel's extensive leisure complex will enable you to work off the excesses of lunch! Booking for the highly popular restaurant is advisable.

MANCHESTER RD., KNUTSFORD, CHESHIRE. Tel: 0565•50333. Fax: 0565•55351

THE LANCASTER RESTAURANT

Terminal Building, Manchester Airport. Tel: (061) 489 3108.
Hours: *Open for breakfast, lunch and dinner from 7am – 10pm.*
Average Prices: *A la Carte £14; Table d'Hote £10.*
Wines: *House wine from £6.65 per bottle.*

For refreshment en route to an exotic location, or just a chance to relax and watch the comings and goings of this busy airport, the Lancaster Restaurant is ideal, its friendly and helpful staff promoting a relaxed atmosphere. Situated within the main airport terminal building, it commands panoramic views of both the airport and Cheshire countryside. Menus are ideal, offering a combination of French and traditional English dishes ranging from the 20 minute range for the traveller in a hurry, a Spiderman and Batman menu for children, to a full à la carte. A selection such as chicken schnitzel, grilled halibut steak or scampi in a three capsicum sauce will enhance the plane spotting. There are also special 'international weeks' sponsored by foreign airlines, when Italian, Greek, Australian and many other worldwide cuisines are available. The wine list complements the international air; it is extensive and features a good selection of worldwide names. All major credit cards are welcome, as are parties.

SAWASDEE THAI RESTAURANT

	Churchgate, Stockport. Tel: (061) 429 0488.
Hours:	*Open for lunch and dinner until 10.30pm. Closed Mon and Sun lunchtimes.*
Average Prices:	*A la Carte £14.*
Wines:	*House wine £6 per bottle.*

Housed in two storeys of an original 1820's Stockport building, the Sawasdee Restaurant offers an enticing combination of authentic Thai cuisine in a very friendly and convivial atmosphere. It is a haven for the lover of Thai food, with waitresses dressed in traditional Thai costume serving in the appropriate manner. The restaurant is decorated in a sympathetic flavour, and the whole is relaxed, there being no time limit on meals — in fact, the management stress that your table will be guaranteed for the night. An authentic Thai cuisine is prepared by Bangkok trained chefs, who advise diners unaccustomed to Thai cuisine. Starters such as house speciality chicken in pan dan leaf or various types of tam yam soups are followed by fish and prawns imported from Thailand and the Bay of Siam. Desserts can be a delicate banana in coconut milk, papaya and melon and a choice of fruits. Thai music completes the ambiance of this restaurant, a place where a simple meal turns into a delightful experience amid tranquil, unhurried surroundings. Most major credit cards accepted.

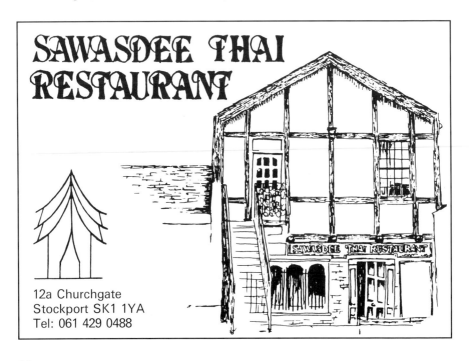

SAWASDEE THAI RESTAURANT

12a Churchgate
Stockport SK1 1YA
Tel: 061 429 0488

THE BRAMHALL MOATHOUSE

Bramhall, Stockport, Cheshire. Tel: (061) 439 8116.

Hours: *Open for lunch, dinner and bar meals until 9.45pm.*

Average Prices: *A la Carte £20; Table d'Hôte £12.95.*

Wines: *House wine £7.95 per bottle.*

Owned by Queen's Moat Houses, this refurbished hotel has the combined attractions of an inviting French and English cuisine and a pleasant restaurant in which to enjoy it. Guests can pause for a leisurely aperitif in the County Bar, whilst soft background music will relax the diner in the County restaurant, tastefully decorated in pastel pinks and blues. Chef Jeff Peach prepares a daily changing table d'hôte, and seasonally changing à la carte from which diners can choose starters of chicken fumé (batons of smoked chicken and melon in a chervil vinaigrette), gravadlax with dill or Pear au Maigret (cinnamon poached pear and roast Maigret duck fanned out on a light fruit coulis), before moving to main dishes of monkfish Thermidor, fillet of lamb en croûte or perhaps escalope of salmon with a hollandaise sauce. Alternatively, the bar serves traditional food — steak and kidney pie, sandwiches and soup, all cooked freshly to order. Special facilities and adapted bedrooms are provided for the disabled, and vegetarian dishes and children's portions are available on request. Frequent dinner dances add to the fun. All credit cards.

The Bramhall Moat House

Bramhall Lane South
Bramhall, Stockport,
Cheshire.
Telephone: 061·439·8116
Telex: 668464
Fax: 061·440 8071

INTERNATIONAL HOTELIERS

THE THREE GATES RESTAURANT

	Woodford, Stockport. Tel: (061) 440 8715/439 7824
Hours:	*Open for lunch Tues – Fri and dinner Mon – Sat.*
Average Prices:	*A La Carte from £22.*

Discover The Three Gates Restaurant in Woodford, where you will find a full â la carte offering a superb selection of Chef Gary Jenkins' special dishes. Using only fresh produce, he prepares modern British cuisine to a standard reflected in the restaurants two-star Good Food Guide and AA top 50 ratings. All major credit cards.

547 CHESTER RD, WOODFORD, BRAMHALL, CHESHIRE, 061·440·8715   061·439·7824

STANNEYLANDS HOTEL

	Stanneylands Road, Wilmslow. Tel: (0625) 525225.
Hours:	*Open for lunch and dinner until 10pm.*

The combination of a beautiful setting with extensive gardens and a peaceful lake, with a high standard of staff and service creates in this extended Edwardian hotel a charming ambiance for dining. Rooms are attractively furnished with comfortable chairs, oak panels and open fires. The appealing dining room has panelled walls, offset by tables of shining silverware — a setting only enhanced by the inventive and memorable cuisine. High quality ingredients are used; textures and flavours finely judged, and specialities can include roast breast of wild duck with a gigot ballotine, mignons of beef fillet, and fillets of seabass and scallops in a seaweed batter. A very good, wide ranging wine list accompanies — Rioja Alta Reserva 904 '75, Joseph Phelps Chardonnay '80. Payment by credit card is accepted.

SHRIGLEY HALL HOTEL GOLF AND COUNTRY CLUB

Shrigley Park, Pott Shrigley, Macclesfield.
Tel: (0625) 575757.

Hours:	*Open for lunch, dinner and bar meals until 9.45pm.*
Average Prices:	*Table d'Hôte £18; Sun lunch £13.*
Wines:	*House wine £7.50 per bottle.*

In the 260 acre estate of Shrigley Park in East Cheshire, lies this prestigious country club. Built in the 19th century, it was a private house until 1929, when it was sold to the Salesian Order of Missionaries, with whom it remained until the 1980's. In 1989, the Hall was restored to its former grandeur, becoming a stylish English country house hotel, its interior reflecting the many classical features of the original design. Should a day spent playing golf, riding or working out in the hotel's leisure complex leave you in need of refreshment, there are a variety of places in which to dine. The Oakridge Restaurant gives breathtaking views over the hills of the Peak District, whilst chef Peter Walters uses the best of market fresh produce in creating a cuisine which complements the classicism of the hall. To begin with, Cheshire game sausage, or gravadlax of salmon, with perhaps pork, pheasant and bacon for main dishes. Sweets are similarly attractive, but only for those eager to return to the gym! Live music adds to the fun, and most major credit cards are accepted.

The Oakridge Restaurant at Shrigley Hall Hotel, Macclesfield. Tel. (0625) 575757

The LeghArms
and Black Boy Restaurant

FINE CUISINE AND A FINE TRADITION

LUNCHEONS · DINNERS SERVED DAILY
PRESTBURY VILLAGE, CHESHIRE
Tel. Prestbury (0625) 829130 or 827833

LEGH ARMS AND BLACK BOY RESTAURANT

Prestbury Village, near Macclesfield, Cheshire.
Tel: (0625) 829130.

Hours:	*Open for lunch and dinner until 11pm; bar meals except Sun.*
Average Prices:	*A la Carte £16; Sun lunch £9.95.*
Wines:	*House wine £8 per litre.*

A reputation for hospitality which stretches back 500 years has earned this Cheshire village pub renown as a special dining experience. Dating back to the fifteenth century, the building was originally called The Saracen's Head, but a sign painter unfamiliar with Saracens painted a negro's head instead, and it became known as the Blackamoor's Head, and later the Black Boy. The inn's earliest claim to fame came in 1745, when it was host to one Charles Edward Stuart, 'Bonnie Prince Charlie' of Scottish fame, who passed through the village on his ill-fated bid to snatch the throne of England. On reaching Derby, however, he was sent back to Scotland to be defeated at the Battle of Culloden. Nowadays, rebellion of any kind is definitely NOT encouraged, and the weary traveller, Scotsman or otherwise, is assured of a warm welcome and a peaceful experience, whether the order is a simple bar snack, a casual meal in the Black Boy Bistro, or an evening dinner in the Legh Arms restaurant. Longstanding tenants Otto and Mavis Polyanszky employ a cosmopolitan staff to ensure that their avowed aim of providing classical English and French cuisine with service which is 'friendly, quiet, unobtrusive and highly efficient' is achieved. Head chef Yannick Herin prepares both à la carte and table d'hôte menus, offering a wide choice — select from the seafood starters before dining on perhaps a braised partridge served with grapes and apple purées, or other seasonal game, with a sliced mango and papaya to conclude. A choice from the vintage wines will complement a dénouement from the cheeseboard. Alternatively, hot and cold bar snacks are also available lunchtimes and every evening except Saturday, but, either way, staff endeavour to make the dining experience as pleasant and comfortable as possible. An extra addition to the inn gives a new link with an old tradition — the Legh Arms now has a bar-be-que and beer garden, which has been given the name of......The Saracen's Bar! All major credit cards.

MOTTRAM HALL HOTEL

Mottram St. Andrew, Prestbury, Cheshire.
Tel: (0625) 828135.

Hours:	*Open for lunch and dinner. Rest. closed Sat lunch.*
Average Prices:	*A la Carte £23; Sun lunch £13.*
Wines:	*House wine £9.75 per bottle.*

Built in 1721 by Nathaniel Booth, this imposing hall has over 300 acres of parkland to ensure privacy and yet is only ten minutes drive from the nearby M56. It provides a fine example of Georgian architecture, in particular the beautifully restored Adam ceilings in the Cocktail Bar, and fine classical fireplace of the lounge. With full conference function facilities, plus 95 luxurious bedrooms, it makes an ideal location for business and private parties, and frequently bustles with visitors to the leisure club. The Georgian Restaurant offers an extensive à la carte or daily changing table d'hôte selection. Chef de Cuisine, Ian Myers, prepares imaginative English/French dishes — starters of 'Mushrooms Mottram Hall' (button mushroom cups filled with crabmeat and prawns) may be followed by Beef St Jacques (strips of beef fillet cooked in a brandy, wine and lobster sauce). Mouthwatering desserts freshly prepared on the premises conclude, and children's menus and vegetarian dishes are available on request. Saturday night dinner dances add to the fun, whilst garden entertainments should expend any excess energy. All major cards.

SILKS RESTAURANT AND TEA SHOP

SILKS RESTAURANT and TEA SHOP

The Heritage Centre
Roe Street
Macclesfield

Telephone: 0625 613572

THE STANLEY ARMS

Macclesfield Forest, near Wildboarclough, Macclesfield.
Tel: (02605) 2414.

Hours: *Open for lunch, 12 – 2.30pm, and dinner (last orders 10pm),*
                     and bar meals.

Average Prices: *A la Carte £12; bar meals from £5.*

Wines: *House wines from £5.95 per bottle.*

This Marstons' pub is to be found in a building of finest Cheshire/Derbyshire
stone, amidst picturesque surroundings. It offers good traditional English and
French cuisine, with personal service in a warm friendly atmosphere. The
extensive à la carte menu can be sampled either in the separate restaurant —
its inviting open fire illuminating a cosy room adorned with handpainted
watercolours, fresh flowers and hand-painted pottery — or in the dining room.
Chef Alan Harvey has wide experience as a head chef throughout Europe, and
brings to his dishes flair and style. Choose from perhaps a dressed Scottish
crab, or king prawns in garlic mushrooms as starters to house speciality
ducklings, or a Scottish salmon with scallops and prawns baked in fillo pastry.
The sweet-trolley will only leave you wanting more — exotic ice creams,
Blackforest gateaux, and chocolate fudge cake are to be enjoyed. Both children
and vegetarians are catered for, and all diners are welcome to ask for any dish
not on the menu. As well as the many excellent European wines, real ales are
served. Private parties are welcome.

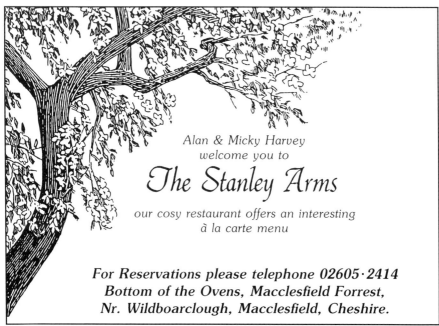

GREAT MORETON HALL HOTEL

	New Road, Congleton, Cheshire. Tel: (0260) 272340.
Hours:	*Open for coffee, tea and dinner until 9.30pm.*
Average Prices:	*A la Carte £22; Table d'Hôte £15.*
Wines:	*House wine £7.95 per bottle.*

The combination of tasteful elegance, beautiful surroundings and friendly service makes this a gem of an hotel. Designed by Victorian architect Edward Blore, this magnificent Revival Gothic Manor has been restored to its former glory and transformed into a luxurious country house hotel. Its serenely beautiful 45 acres of park and woodlands reflect the irresistible relaxation and grace found within the hotel. Ideally located for visiting the historic towns of Cheshire, hotel staff are ready and willing to advise on sightseeing trips, whilst nearby courses will keep golfers happy. The luxurious restaurant serves a traditional English cuisine, with the best of local produce used to prepare perhaps marinated salmon Great Moreton, fillet of sea bass or goose breast, complemented by a large selection of fine vintage wines and ports. An experienced staff ensures that the guest's every need is met, whilst two well-appointed suites are available for private functions, conferences or dances. A weekly pianist provides a subtle refrain whilst you dine. All major credit cards.

41

THE YELLOW BROOM RESTAURANT

Twemlow Green, Near Holmes Chapel, Cheshire.
Tel: (0477) 33289.

Hours: *Open for lunch and dinner (last orders 10.30pm).*
                         Restaurant is closed on Sunday evenings and Mondays.

The renowned Yellow Broom Restaurant is situated in a picturesque setting in the small country village of Twemlow Green on the main road from Macclesfield to Holmes Chapel. The restaurant is owned and exquisitely run by Renate Pola and her manager Martin Jones, who are both very experienced and enthusiastic restauranteurs. This charming establishment with its elegant furnishings and decor accommodates up to fifty diners in a really delightful ambience and the luxurious cocktail bar is just the place to enjoy an aperitif whilst selecting dishes from the superb menu of French cuisine. Top chef M. Francis Gonnard and his staff prepare and present the food with very appealing flair and in addition to the current evening menu he has gained an enviable reputation for traditional sunday lunches. The Yellow Broom Restaurant regularly features leading cabaret stars such as Iris Williams, Vince Hill and Tony Christie. Business parties and conferences can be booked by arrangement. Settlement of accounts by credit cards is welcomed.

THE YELLOW BROOM RESTAURANT
Twemlow Green, Nr. Holmes Chapel, Cheshire. Tel: 0477-33289

THE OLD VICARAGE HOTEL

Cranage, Holmes Chapel, Cheshire. Tel: (0477) 32041.

Hours:	*Open for coffee; Riverside Restaurant open for lunch and dinner until 10pm. Vestry Bistro open for lunch and dinner, seven days a week.*
Average Prices:	*A la Carte £15; Sun lunch £9.*
Wines:	*House wine £8 per bottle.*

Antiquity and elegance are the hallmarks of this 17th century Grade Two listed building. Situated by the riverside at Cranage, it is surrounded by beautiful Cheshire countryside and places of interest. Historic Chester and the castles at Beeston and Cholmondeley, Georgian cotton mills, and breathtaking views over Cheshire from Alderley Edge — all are within easy reach. Should you not wish to venture from the warm and cosy hotel, there are 23 comfortable and stylish bedrooms, and an attractive restaurant where an imaginative high quality English and French cuisine can be sampled. Alternatively, with its original inglenook fireplace and oak-beamed ceilings, the Vestry Bistro will prompt a sojourn in past times. Here, a wide choice of delicious hot and cold dishes are available. With the emphasis on the enjoyment and uniqueness of the guest, the Old Vicarage caters for one to 80 with equal care and consideration. Modified bedrooms are provided for the disabled, and children are most welcome. Credit cards welcome.

The Old Vicarage Hotel

**Cranage, Holmes Chapel, Cheshire
Tel. (0477) 32041. Fax (0477) 35728**

ROOKERY HALL

	Worleston, near Nantwich. Tel: (0270) 626866.
Hours:	*Open for coffee, lunch and dinner until 9.45pm.*
Average Prices:	*A la Carte £30; Sun lunch £18.*
Wines:	*House wine £13 per bottle.*

Beautiful parkland with lakes and fountains make an idyllic setting for this striking Georgian house. Built as the home of a wealthy landowner, it was purchased in 1867 by Baron William Von Schroder, who transformed it into a small chateau, giving it its unusual Continental character. To the front, it is graced by sweeping lawns leading to a lake; to the rear, a magnificent terrace overlooks a large fountain and lawn. Yet, the external attractions do not detract from the character and style of the interior. The hall boasts elegant day rooms and a splendid Victorian dining room, hand cut crystal glass and fine bone china adding that touch of elegance, fully reflecting the quality of the English/French cuisine. Manager David Tearle extends a warm welcome, whilst the chef prepares perhaps terrine of Cumbrian rabbit, fillet of Scotch beef or marinated scallops, concluded by a noteworthy English cheeseboard. To complement the renowned cuisine, the Hall boasts an exciting wine list — many good Californian wines, vintage burgundies, clarets and ports to tempt the palate of the discerning. Vegetarians catered for, and eleven luxury bedrooms. All credit cards.

ROOKERY HALL

Worleston, Nr. Nantwich, Cheshire CW5 6DQ. Tel. (0270) 626866
Telex: 367169   Fax: 0270-626027

ARKLE RESTAURANT AT THE CHESTER GROSVENOR HOTEL

	Eastgate Street, Chester. Tel: (0244) 324024
Hours:	*Open for lunch Tues – Sat and dinner Mon – Sat (last orders 10pm). Closed Sunday.*
Average Prices:	*Lunch £17.50; Dinner £40.*

The beautiful, historic city of Chester boasts many fine buildings and monuments — the Chester Grosvenor, with its stately half-timbered facade, is one of its landmarks. A striking Library bar charms with its book selection, muted lighting and evening piano music, ideal for quiet socialising whilst awaiting dinner. The restaurant itself is small and intimate, its walls adorned with many original paintings and the focal point is an atrium with a large weeping fig tree. A delightful setting for the imaginatively prepared modern cuisine. Lunchtime sees a wide fixed-price menu, and in the evening delicacies such as an aspic of citrus fruits with melon pearls, and a cutlet of duckling with Chinese style scampi tails suggest themselves. Desserts are inviting and might be a fine biscuit with poached pear and hazelnut caramel. Should you wish to extend your stay, there are 86 impressive bedrooms, whilst the excesses of dining can be worked off in the hotel's gymnasium.

ABBEY GREEN RESTAURANT

	Abbey Green, Northgate Street, Chester. Tel: (0244) 313251
Hours:	*Open for lunch and dinner (last orders 10.15pm).*
Average Prices:	*Table d'Hôte £12.50 (dinner) £5 (lunch).*
Wines:	*House wine £6.50 per bottle.*

Voted the National Vegetarian Restaurant of 1988/1989, and "Good Food Guide's" County Restaurant of the Year, the Abbey Green has been completely refurbished, with new tableware and a landscaped garden for summer dining, as well as a new lilac and pink decor. The restaurant is itself on the ground floor of a pretty house, and diners can study the menu by a coal fire in a small, intimate lounge before removing to the welcoming restaurant. The cuisine is a wholesome delight for vegetarians; well-balanced and full of surprises. A wide choice offers perhaps pasta polynesia, avocado crêpe with lime sauce, and imam bayeldi (Turkish stuffed aubergines). Imaginative combinations result: peanut sauce covers pasta polynesia, green pasta layers pineapple avocado and ginger. An accompanying wine list is interesting, and reasonably priced, with some very good organic labels, and cellarman's choice Montana Sauvignon 1987. Children and parties are welcome, and its ground floor location facilitates disabled dining. Access and Visa.

CRABWALL MANOR HOTEL

Mollington, Chester. Tel: (0244) 851666.

Hours:	*Open for lunch and dinner (last orders 9.30pm).*
Average Prices:	*A la Carte £30; Table d'Hôte £21.*
Wines:	*House wine £8.95 per bottle.*

Blissful it would be if all hotels retained that reminder of much lamented days of complete luxury and faultless service which Crabwall does. Set in 11 acres of gardens and parkland just minutes from Chester, Crabwall is an early 19th century Tudor/Gothic style castellated manor house, its imposing clock tower watches new arrivals as they are relieved of their luggage. Inside, the decor is timeless — beautiful fabrics and subtle lighting are warm and inviting, and there is a choice of drawing room, cocktail bar, or Inglenook with adjoining snooker room in which to relax before removing to the restaurant. Under the capable hands of ex-Box Tree chef Michael Truelove, a combination of modern and traditional English cuisine is served. Menus are changed weekly, but examples might be a terrine of assorted game, roast breast of chicken served with langoustines, or fresh hake with the enticing Charlotte au chocolat to conclude. There are some very good wines chosen with knowledge — Savigny les Beaune (Bize) 1983, Hermitage la Chapelle 1980 — to appeal to the discerning, whilst the pianist plays softly in the background. Excellent facilities for the disabled.

CRABWALL MANOR
HOTEL · AND · RESTAURANT

Parkgate Road,
Mollington, Chester CH1 6NE

Tel (0244) 851666
Fax (0244) 851400

NUNSMERE HALL HOTEL AND RESTAURANT

Sandiway, Cheshire. Tel: (0606) 889100.

Hours: *Open for coffee, lunch, afternoon tea and dinner. Last orders 9.30pm.*

Average Prices: *Table d'hôte Lunch £15.50; Sunday lunch £12.00; Table d'hôte Dinner £25.00.*

Wines: *House wine £8.25 per bottle.*

Set on a peninsula in ten acres of countryside, almost surrounded by a large lake, this makes a beautiful location for this family run hotel. Priding itself on its high standards and personal service, it offers all the atmosphere and hospitality of a country house amidst the peace and quiet of beautiful Cheshire countryside. Built in 1898 for Lord Brocklebank (one of the founders of the Cunard steamship company), it has been sympathetically restored by present owners Malcolm and Julie McHardy. It is ideal for both conferences or a relaxing weekend; close to the city of Chester, two famous golf courses, and a racing circuit, Nunsmere also has ten acres of wooded grounds. The cuisine is an integral part of the hotel's appeal: an imaginative traditional/modern English style provides interesting and varied starters to complement the main course such as Welsh lamb with creamed leeks and fillet of beef with morels and a rich red wine sauce, roast pheasant or wild salmon perhaps. A varied and interesting wine list ensures a quality accompaniment to the meal.

NUNSMERE HALL

TARPORLEY RD
SANDIWAY
CHESHIRE
CW8 2ES
Tel: 0606·889100

THE RHEINGOLD RIVERSIDE INN

Acton Bridge, near Northwich, Cheshire. Tel: (0606) 852310.

Hours:	*Open for lunch, dinner and bar snacks until 9.30pm. Closed Sun/Mon except for bar snacks.*
Average Prices:	*A la Carte £14; snacks from £1.50.*
Wines:	*House wine from £5.25 per bottle.*

A dreamy location on the banks of the River Weaver makes this an attractive venue for that special occasion. This restaurant is tastefully decorated with candlelit tables and fresh flowers, creating an elegant air which the soft lilting tones of the pianist only enhance. A large delightfully furnished conservatory, with mesmeric riverside views, is ideal for weddings and photos, whilst the inn has its own changing room for such occasions. Enjoy a quiet pre-dinner drink at the Piano Bar — perhaps a choice of one of the hundreds of cocktails — and peruse the international menu. The kitchen prepares oysters and escargots Bretagne or sevruga Russian caviar for starters, before a main course of perhaps scampi Provençale, duck à l'orange, or coquilles St. Jacques Parisienne, complemented by a suitably international wine list. Well-known as a venue for office parties, business lunches and other speciality occasions, The Riverside also has weekly dinner dances, and menus tailored for parties of 15 or more. Visa and Access.

49

LA GRANDE BOUFFE

Castle Street, Liverpool. Tel: (051) 236 3375.

Hours: *Open for coffee, lunch and dinner until 10.30pm. Closed Sun.*
Average Prices: *A la Carte £16.*
Wines: *House wine £5.50 per bottle.*

At the heart of Liverpool city centre, this Grade Two listed building makes an engaging basement brasserie. During the day it bustles with activity, reverting by nightfall to a more sophisticated style. The interior is decorated with church pews and Singer sewing machines, yet jazz music and 40's and 50's female vocalists suggest a latent but irresistible wildness and originality. The style is also reflected in the cuisine — longstanding ex-Munich chef Terry Lewis brings a French flair to starters of fish soups and terrines, main dishes of perhaps wild duck with honey and peppercorns, and the wide variety of fish and game dishes. Traditional English food comes to the fore on the sweet-trolley, though — sticky toffee pudding or brandied bread and butter pudding amongst others. An expanded and developed wine list now represents most of the major regions — a treat for the connoisseur, as are the frequent wine promotion evenings — Beaujolais, Valentines, Bastille. Vegetarians and children are catered for, and most major cards are accepted.

La Grande Bouffe

Déjeuner Dîner Souper

48A Castle Street
Liverpool L2 7LQ
telephone 051-236 3375

THE PARK HOTEL

Netherton, Merseyside. Tel: (051) 525 7555.

Hours: *Open for lunch and dinner until 9.30pm, and bar meals. Closed Sat lunch.*

Average Prices: *A la Carte £11; Sun lunch £6.95.*

The city of Liverpool, Aintree racecourse, airports and motorways are minutes from this well-appointed hotel. Dishes are traditional, with a French flair — chicken bordelaise and scampi Provençale (cooked at your table) . Conferences and banquets are the hotel's forte, but staff ensure that whatever the occasion, your stay will prove a memorable one. Payment by credit card is accepted.

PEKING DUCK RESTAURANT

Smithdown Road, Liverpool. Tel: (051) 733 0723.

Hours: *Open for dinner 5.30pm – 12.30am. Closed Tuesday.*

Average Prices: *Good quality value for money prices.*

For a taste of Chinese food in Liverpool, come to this traditional Peking restaurant! Decorated in a Tudor style, the atmosphere is warm and friendly and makes for a relaxing meal. Special seafood banquets are an added attraction, and private parties are welcome. Young lovers of Peking cuisine will not be put off — the restaurant caters for children. Visa and Access are accepted.

ARMADILLO

20 – 22 Matthew Street, Liverpool. Tel: (051) 236 4123.

Hours: *Open Tues – Sat for lunch and dinner until 10.30pm. Closed Sun and Mon.*

Average Prices: *Table d'Hôte £6.95.*

Wines: *House wine £6 per bottle.*

Escape from the hustle and bustle of Liverpool City at this modern café-cum-restaurant, on the same street as the legendary Cavern Club. Light, bright, yet very relaxing, it extends a welcoming and enthusiastic ambiance, and staff serve a wide variety of dishes, ranging from stuffed quail and confit of duck with cranberries to red mullet with pesto and pheasant with cream, and venison olives with Madeira sauce. Desserts continue the quality, and there are some enjoyable vegetarian dishes. Lunchtime and pre-theatre set menus offer very good value for money, whilst lunch is served non-stop from 11.45am to 5pm on Saturday. A fine wine list accompanies, compiled by a real enthusiast: Marques de Grinon Cabernet Sauvignon 1982. Children's helpings available on request. Payment by Access is accepted.

ELHAM

Renshaw Street, Liverpool. Tel: (051) 709 1589.

Hours: *Open for dinner 7pm – 2.30am, until 3.30am Fri and Sat.*

Average Prices: *A la Carte £10.*

Highly recommended by the Good Food Guide for five consecutive years, and voted Best Middle Eastern and Steak Restaurant in Liverpool in 1986, the Elham is well worth sampling. The cuisine alone — mixture of Lebanese and charcoal grill dishes — is engaging, and perfectly matches the restful decor and warm, relaxing atmosphere. A 12 course banquet will delight lovers of Middle Eastern cuisine.

ELHAM

**95 Renshaw Street
Liverpool
L1 2SP
Tel: 051 709 1589**

Moreton

The No 1 Hotel
For your Business Functions and Conferences

*We specialise in Weddings, Conferences and Ladies Nights.
Contact us and talk it through, let us help make your event a success.*

For the best in Bar Lunch Food.
Or just a Jacket Potato from as little as 95 pence.
MONDAY TO SATURDAY; NOON TILL 3 pm.

For the finest Food and the finest Value
why not try our Fabulous
4-Course Dinner at only 10.90
Mon-Fri 7pm-9.30 Last Orders.
Or
Traditional Sunday Lunch 7.25. Children 3.95.
Or
Sunday Dinner 5-Courses 11.80

MONDAY *Dance Night* **TUESDAY** *Trad Jazz*
WEDNESDAY *Big Band Night - Listen and Dance*
THURSDAY *Country and Western*

BAR OPEN TO THE PUBLIC

Leasowe Castle Hotel

& CONFERENCE CENTRE

1st Junction M53 Motorway. 1 mile Leasowe, Moreton Wirral.
Telephone 051-606 9191. Telex 627 189 Castle

54

BEADLES

Oxton, Birkenhead. Tel: (051) 653 9010.

Hours: *Open for dinner 7.30 – midnight. Closed Sun/Mon.*

Average Prices: *A la Carte £15 (last orders 9pm).*

Wines: *House wine £5.50 per bottle.*

Proprietors Roy and Bea Gott welcome the Merseyside diner to their intimate and unusual restaurant. Highly recommended for its good bistro food, attentive service and 'splendid Black Puddings', the restaurant ensures personal service, and food is well thought out and served. Bea offers variety within a monthly changing menu, with dishes ranging from the simple — melon and Parma ham — across a range of national influences, as in first courses of nori roulade, tabouleh and brandade de cabillaud — to traditional and modern British ideas. Main courses offer perhaps a game pie, and calf's liver, with favourite treacle lick as a typical pudding. Background music relaxes, whilst an enthusiastically chosen wine list (cellarman's choice Morgon and Domaine Les Pillets), and unlimited coffee accompanies. Children are welcome, and wheelchair access (one step) facilitates disabled dining.

TREE TOPS COUNTRY HOUSE RESTAURANT

Woodvale, Formby. Tel: (07048) 79651.

Hours: *Open for coffee, lunch and dinner and bar meals until 9.30pm.*

Average Prices: *A la Carte £16; snacks from £1.75.*

Look no further for that place of rest and recuperation! Close to the beach and golfcourses, yet only minutes from Southport and Liverpool, Tree Tops is a haven of tranquillity. Dine on the renowned English and French cuisine amidst chandeliers and crystal glasses, or perhaps sip an aperitif in the Cocktail Lounge whilst overlooking the swimming pool. High standard chalet accommodation is available in the woodland grounds, and weddings and dinner dances are a speciality. Major cards.

SQUIRES RESTAURANT

King Street, Southport, Lancs. Tel: (0704) 30046.
Hours: *Open for dinner until 10.30pm, and Sun lunch.*
Average Prices: *A la Carte £22; Sun lunch £12.*

Housed in a Victorian building within Southport's premier shopping centre, Squires is an enchanting family-run restaurant, boasting an open seawashed brick fireplace. Walls adorned with an interesting collection of prints and paintings offset tables decorated with fresh flowers and candles. Such style is designed for a relaxing, intimate evening, complemented by the highest quality food. The restaurant offers a fine classic French cuisine, rich with seafood and steaks — daily fresh lobster, finest Scottish salmon and Tournedos Rossini among others. To complement the meal, the discerning guest can select from an extensive wine list which includes many fine Chateau bottled names. Catering for parties is a speciality of Squires when menus are formulated to meet specific requirements. Such is also the case with those of a non meat-eating disposition. All major credit cards are accepted, and children are welcome.

Squires

78–80 KING STREET
SOUTHPORT
PR8 1LS

TELEPHONE
SOUTHPORT
(0704)
30046

MAWDSLEYS EATING HOUSE

Mawdesley, near Ormskirk, Lancs.
Tel: (0704) 822552/821874.

Hours: *Open for coffee, lunch and dinner until 10pm; bar meals except Sun.*

Average Prices: *A la Carte £12.*

In the picturesque village of Mawdesley (recently voted Lancashire's 'Best Kept Village'), lies Mawdsleys Eating House. Prior to being the Towngate Basket Works, this warm and friendly establishment was a farm, and whilst standing in the lounge bar, you are in the area where cattle stood over a hundred years ago. Dining nowadays is much more civilised, however, and since its renovation in 1982, the restaurant exudes an impressive and attractive aura. An interesting cuisine may start with hot seafood pancake, halibut, cockles and mussels, with perhaps a steak Diane or venison. A wide choice of vegetarian dishes is on offer, and some delicious home made sweets. The characterful lounge is a pleasant place in which to sample coffee — the Mawdsley 'special' with Grand Marnier and Tia Maria is tempting — and a fine selection of hand made chocolates. Mawdsley's also caters for parties, weddings and other celebratory events, and welcomes all credit cards.

MAWDSLEYS EATING HOUSE, HALL LN, MAWDESLEY, NR. ORMSKIRK. Tel: 0704 822552/821874

THE CROMWELLIAN

	Kirkham, Preston. Tel: (0772) 685680.
Hours:	*Open for dinner Tues – Sat (last orders 9.30pm) and Sunday lunch. Closed Mon eve.*
Average Prices:	*Table d'Hôte £18; Sun lunch £11.*
Wines:	*House wine £6.95 per bottle.*

Nestling between a green-grocery shop and a taxi firm on Kirkham's main street, is this small restaurant of increasing popularity. Housed in a building which dates back to the 1660's, the Cromwellian impresses both by its warmth and its frequent mentions in national food guides. Its owners Peter and Josie Fawcett have literally started from scratch; prior to taking over the Cromwellian in 1986, neither had any experience in running a restaurant. Yet, their enthusiasm has paid off — standards as well as business are rising. A monthly changing menu utilises the best of seasonal ingredients in the preparation of modern British dishes. Chef Josie serves starters of filo pastry with cream cheese, or broccoli and fennel soup before perhaps trout, chicken breast and salmon with white wine. Desserts will leave you wanting more — butterscotch meringue pie, spiced apple cheesecake and so on. The mostly French wine list is, like the restaurant, gradually expanding, and children and vegetarians are catered for. With three separate dining rooms, the Cromwellian is ideal for parties and business meetings. Credit cards accepted.

The Cromwellian

16 POULTON ST, KIRKHAM, PRESTON, LANCS. PR4 2AB. Tel 0772 685680

EL NIDO

Whinney Brow, A6 Forton, Nr Garstang, Preston.
Tel: (0524) 791254.

Hours:
Open for dinner 7–10.15pm. Closed Mon. Lunch every Wed–Fri, 12–2pm, May–Sept and Dec. Sunday lunch throughout the year.

Average Prices: *A la Carte £15; Lunch £7.*

Wines: *House wine from £6.50 per bottle.*

For a little Puerto Banus in the heart of Lancashire, René and Tracey Mollinga invite you to this, their typically Spanish restaurant. Located one mile from junction 33 of the M6, El Nido brings a cosmopolitan flavour to the fringes of the fylde country. The extensive menu stretches through typical Spanish country dishes to more sophisticated, familiar international cuisine. Feel the atmosphere of Spain whilst dining on Pollo Natalia — chicken breast stuffed with bananas, pineapple and mushrooms, flambéed in brandy or Solomillo El Nido — fillet steak in shallots, artichokes and herbs with a wine and brandy sauce. You can also sample more traditional dishes of Paella, Rabbit or stuffed or fried Squid. Conclude with a home-made sweet or Spanish fruit ice-cream. All dishes are complemented by a wide selection of Rioja, French, Italian and German wines. Sunday lunch offers a traditional three course table d'hote menu, and a 'little Amigos' menu for the children. Live music every Friday. Access and Visa welcome.

WHINNEY BROW
FORTON
NR. GARSTANG
PRESTON
PR3 0AE
Tel: 0524-791254

SWALLOW TRAFALGAR HOTEL

Samlesbury, Preston. Tel: (0772) 877351.

Hours:	*Restaurant open for lunch and dinner until 9.30pm (9pm on Sundays). Closed for Sat lunch. Pub lunches seven days a week 12–2pm.*
Average Prices:	*Dinner £11.95; Lunch £7.75.*
Wines:	*House wine £7 per bottle.*

Formerly named The Five Barred Gate, this Swallow Hotel owned eating-place has been extensively upgraded and refurbished in recent years. One of the latest features among the many additions is 'The Swallow Leisure Club', an extensive complex featuring sauna, steam room, swimming pool and multi gym. The cuisine is equally extensive, with the Trafalgar Restaurant offering an international menu with dishes from as far apart as Lancashire and China. Starters range from Crab Rangoon to Arkwright's Chicken salad, and main courses can be Supreme Gornall, Shish Touk, or perhaps the intriguing Escallopes of Salmon Samantha. Alternatively, the bar can cater for the lunchtime diner in a hurry, with a variety of wholesome pub grub. Children are welcome in the restaurant, and can select from a special menu. The Swallow thoughtfully provides a disabled person's washroom, whilst the restaurant itself has a ramp access. Live music adds that extra ingredient to dining out and may be arranged for private parties either in the restaurant or in one of the banqueting suites. All major credit cards are accepted as payment.

SAMLESBURY, PRESTON, PR5 0UL. Tel. 0772·877351. Fax: 0772·877424

THE RIVER HOUSE

Skippool Creek, Thornton-Le-Fylde, near Blackpool.
Tel: (0253) 883497/883307.

Hours: *Open for lunch and dinner (last orders 9pm).*
Average Prices: *A la Carte £28.*
Wines: *House wine £10.50 per bottle.*

'Having a meal at the River House is the second most pleasurable thing that a man and woman can enjoy!' exclaims host Bill Scott. Many would agree with him, for tucked away among the small yachts and wooden landings at Skippool Creek, lies one of the most famous and popular watering holes in Lancashire. Built in 1830, the River House exudes warmth and charm, evoking memories of and appreciation for everything a hotel should be — a quiet and friendly home from home. Bill and wife Carole have run the hotel since 1982, and in the restaurant Bill draws on an exciting and varied experience to create a high quality English cuisine. Fish from Fleetwood and pheasant from Bowland Moors are used to prepare a wide selection of seafood and game dishes — fresh scallops, breast of mallard, salmon en croûte concluded by River House Ticky Tacky, and home made sorbets and ice creams, all complemented by a connoisseur's wine list. Should the attraction of beautiful surroundings, fine food and jovial hosts prove too tempting, four delightful rooms are available. Visa and Access.

THE RIVER HOUSE

COUNTRY HOUSE: HOTEL AND RESTAURANT
SKIPOOL CREEK, THORNTON-LE-FYLDE. FY5 5LF
TEL. (0253) 883497/883307

THE INN AT WHITEWELL

	Forest of Bowland, Nr Clitheroe, Lancs. Tel: (02008) 222.
Hours:	*Open for coffee, lunch, dinner and bar meals until 9.30pm.*
Average Prices:	*A la Carte £21. Table d'hote £15.50.*
Wines:	*House wine from £5.90 per bottle.*

Lancashire's beautiful Forest of Bowland provides the setting for this ancient stone inn. Whilst enjoying views across the River Hodder, guests can chat with friends in the tap room, whilst books and paintings provide company in the peaceful lounge. Friendly staff ensure a hearty welcome, and a delightfully mellow dining room provides the venue for Chef, Adrian Sedden's French/traditional dishes. Starters can be Coniston cold smoked trout, smoked duck breast or a homemade soup, before main course of perhaps Chateaubriand, cannon of lamb with its own kidneys and for dessert try tempting hot toffee and syrup sponge, bread and butter pudding and chocolate brandy slab cake, as well as a few of the award winning selection of British Farmhouse cheeses. Alternatively, the bar serves more 'ad hoc' meals such as Cumberland sausage, fisherman's pie and old favourite steak and kidney pie. Hungry youngsters and vegetarians have their own choices, and the real ales will quench a greater thirst. Dining is enhanced by the background refrain of a weekly pianist, and larger parties are welcome. There is a large garden, and coarse and game fishing can be enjoyed in the grounds. Most major cards.

THE AUCTIONEER RESTAURANT

New Market Street, Clitheroe. Tel: (0200) 27153.

Hours: *Open for coffee, lunch and dinner until 9.30pm. Closed during Jan and July.*

Average Prices: *Four course dinner £14; Sun lunch £9; weekday lunch from £4.25.*

Wines: *House wine £6.75 per bottle.*

Chef proprietor Henk Van Heumen draws on his wealth of experience, gained during nine years at The Foxfields, to create a stylish restaurant full of Dutch flair. Centrally located in this market town, The Auctioneer is housed in a Victorian cottage style building, whose interior is made cosy by a log burning fire, brass covered beams and wood carved bar, with Dutch paintings, embroidery and fresh flowers adding a touch of quaint elegance. Service is professional, and smartly dressed staff serve the best of fresh local produce. The style is French, yet tinged with Nouvelle Cuisine, and presentation is noteworthy. Begin with the Dutch appetiser 'Bitterballen' (minced veal in a cream sauce, breadcrumbed and deep fried), with seasonal fresh fish and game to follow, and perhaps a homemade soup. The wine list is impressive, with over 80 worldwide varieties, whilst there are also draught beers. Private parties are catered for, whilst this year sees the start of speciality French evenings, concentrating on all the major regions — a must for lovers of things Continental! Access and Visa accepted.

HENK & FRANCES VAN HEUMEN

NEW MARKET STREET
CLITHEROE BB7 2JW
LANCASHIRE

Tel: 0200 27153

THE CALF'S HEAD HOTEL

	Worston, Clitheroe. Tel: (0200) 41218.
Hours:	*Open for coffee, lunch and dinner until 9.30pm every day except Sunday lunch, when hot meat sandwiches are served from 'The Calfery'.*
Average Prices:	*Very competitive prices.*
Wines:	*House wine £6.95 per litre.*

Nestling peacefully in the historic village of Worston, The Calf's Head unites superb location with comparable standards of service and cuisine. The village itself is interesting — legend has it that the notorious 'Dame Demdyke' weaved her magic spells in one of its cottages, and the remains of a bull ring have been discovered nearby. The magnificent River Ribble and Pendle Hill provide the setting, whilst the inn itself boasts its own picturesque walled garden — a delightful place in the warmth of summer sun, whilst an evening spent before bright glowing fires provides a retreat from the bracing country air in winter. An intimate dining room offers extensive and varied menus to suit all tastes — cooking is both traditional and Continental, with perhaps steak Diane, barbecued loin of local lamb and other delicacies of local produce. Sunday visitors to the hotel can enjoy the 'Hot Calfery', a notable lunchtime roast such as only Lancashire can produce. Dinner dances and champagne evenings add to the fun. Vegetarians and children are catered for. Real ale.

THE DOG AND PARTRIDGE

Wellgate, Clitheroe, Lancs. Tel: (0200) 22465.

Hours: *Open for bar meals, lunch and evenings until 11pm.*

Average Prices: *Snacks from £1.50; meals from £3.*

Ghostly goings on are afoot in this, the oldest pub in Clitheroe! The old beamed ceilings and traditional decor of this former coaching house lend truth to the rumour of a ghost. Yet the hauntings of the past should not stop you enjoying the weekly discos, and speciality evenings of the present. Real ales are available, whilst traditional home fare is the pub's speciality. Ample car parking.

65

BROWN'S BISTRO

Clitheroe, Blackburn. Tel: (0200) 26928.

Hours:	*Open for lunch and dinner until 10pm. Closed Sunday.*
Average Prices:	*A la Carte £16.*
Wines:	*House wines £5.25 per bottle.*

Deep in the heart of Clitheroe lies this typical French bistro, its wooden floorboards, check tablecloths, wine racks and collection of interesting prints and plaques adding that final touch of Continental authenticity. It is run by father and son team of David and Ian Brown, and David's training at top establishments both at home and in Paris is fully reflected in the style and quality of the bistro and its cuisine. Its reputation as one of the best eating houses in Lancashire comes as no surprise as one witnesses its Continental buzz — truly reminiscent of the real thing. The cuisine is likewise authentic French style — delightful when tasted in this bustling atmosphere. Dine on starters delicious enough to be main courses — scallops au gratin, bouillabaisse, salmon, and avocado prawn. These can be followed by perhaps chicken Kiev, scampi, live lobsters and seasonal game, as well as Angus beef which is always hung to perfection. All desserts are home-made, and the meal can be further complemented by an excellent selection of Continental wines. Should you wish to take full advantage of the atmosphere Visa and Access credit cards are welcomed.

BROWNS BISTRO, 10 YORK ST, CLITHEROE Tel 0200 26928

THE HIDE

Ball Grove Country Park, Colne, Lancashire.
Tel: (0282) 869117.

Hours: *Open for lunch and dinner until 9.30pm. Closed Sun evening.*
Average Prices: *A la Carte £20; Table d'Hôte £10.95.*
Wines: *House wine £6.95 per bottle.*

Located on the Lancashire and Yorkshire border, The Hide lies on the site of the old Tannery. Panoramic views over the lakes and countryside of the Country Park will inspire whilst guests await their meal. A pink and cream restaurant decor is complemented by crystal glassware and silver cutlery, with large leather armchairs in which to relax and reflect on the tasteful meal. The chef prepares a mixed seafood and vegetarian cuisine — sample fillet of Fleetwood sole, roast Aylesbury duckling and a classic rib of Aberdeen Angus. The mouthwatering sweet-trolley has attractions such as coconut menorquina, pêche martinique (ice cream made from a fresh peach, and served in its case), or a selection of sorbets. Those with children will have no problem when choosing a meal — youngsters are well-catered for, and can expend their energy afterwards on the garden amusements. The 'Oak Room' will accommodate up to fifty guests, should a celebration be in order. Payment by credit card is accepted.

BALL GROVE COUNTRY PARK, COLNE, LANCS. Tel: 0282-869117

SPARTH HOUSE

Sparth House

A Taste of Victorian Tradition

Victorian Tea Rooms

The Regency Room

SPARTH HOUSE

Clayton-le-Moors, near Accrington. Tel: (0254) 872263.

Hours: *Open for morning coffee, lunch, afternoon tea and dinner until 9.30pm. Closed Sun evening.*

Average Prices: *A la Carte £18; two course table d'hôte lunch £5.95.*

Wines: *House wine £8 per carafe.*

On entering this majestic house, you will be forgiven for feeling a certain 'déja vu'. The house itself was built during the 1700's amid beautiful wooded grounds, and although the exterior favours the Edwardian age, the interior oak panelled walls festooned with oil paintings and antique figures seem to belong to the elegant and enchanting Victorian era — indeed, time seems to have stood still. Situated on the edge of the Ribble Valley, Sparth House is in easy reach of the Lake District and many more local historic features such as Clitheroe Castle and Whalley Abbey. Its location close to three major motorways is a further boon, making this an ideal place to sojourn for both business and pleasure. Since taking over ownership of the house in 1979, Brenda and Walter have seen it go from strength to strength, from its rather humble start. In 1986, Brenda started a small tea room business in the Oak Room. Such was its reputation that another room was opened up, and a more extensive menu added. Two years later, due to increasing demand, the Alexandria Suite was opened, a tastefully decorated room which can cater for up to 100 people. At present, the house boasts two further large dining rooms as well as four luxurious suites, each individually decorated. The restaurant serves a comprehensive array of expertly prepared modern English dishes, with buffet and grill options available. Select perhaps a saddle of lamb with kidney sauce, a fillet of sea trout, or fresh Whitby crab, concluded by a mouthwatering dessert selection — meringue swans with Chantilly cream, or raspberries Romanoff perhaps. Those with children will not be disappointed — there are menus available for them, as well as facilities for the disabled. Access and Visa are welcomed.

Sparth House
LICENSED HOTEL
Enter the
magical worlde
of years gone bye.

THE FOXFIELDS

Whalley Road, Billington, Blackburn. Tel: (0254) 822556.

Hours: *Open for coffee, lunch, dinner and tea until 9.45pm. Open Sat dinner only — from 7.00pm.*

Average Prices: *A la Carte £22; Sun lunch £10.75.*

Wines: *House wine £7.50 per bottle.*

'Good Food Guide' recommendations and AA awards are not given lightly; a visit to The Foxfields will show the diner why. Ideally situated amidst beautiful countryside at the foot of the Pendle Hills, The Foxfields enjoys a long established reputation for quality and excellence. Specially selected local fresh ingredients are transformed by Andrew Balderson (a chef of international repute, recently of Bermuda and Italy) into a high quality combination of classical French and Modern English cuisine — the daily changing menu offers perhaps breast of wild duck, hot pot of local sporting birds, and beef fillet, as well as exotic dishes such as barracuda! An extensive, worldwide wine list includes labels from the Lebanon and New Zealand, whilst the unusual selection of beers will quench a stronger thirst. Already notable for its reception and banqueting facilities, The Foxfields will become the North's first 'all suite' hotel later this year, when its 28 suites are due for completion. Those with disabilities will find access easy, and all credit cards are accepted.

The Foxfields
Whalley Road., Billington
Nr. Whalley, Blackburn
Lancashire BB6 9HY
Tel: 0254·822556   Fax: 0254·824613

COOKIE'S COFFEE SHOP

George Street, Whalley, near Blackburn. Tel: (0254) 822628.
Hours: *Open for coffee, lunch and tea until 4.30pm. Closed Sun.*

Amongst the clothes, millinery, handbags and other ladies' wear at Maureen Cookson's clothes shop, you will find this small but — for the weary shopper — highly essential coffee shop. Located in the pretty village of Whalley in the Ribble Valley, with a Norman church calmly watching over the proceedings, the clothes shop houses this charming eating place. Opened three years ago and situated on the first floor of the shop, Cookies' caters for both customers and the general public. Six days a week, its staff of two prepare a cuisine ranging from fruit loaf and almond quiche to freshly cooked salmon salad, smoked haddock creams, and buttered shrimps. There is always a monthly speciality dish, and a slimmers' lunch, as well as vegetarian dishes. Shoppers with disabilities will be relieved to find a lift to take them to the coffee shop. Once there, both they and other diners can relax in wicker chairs, whilst gazing through a glass wall onto bustling shoppers. Its necessary proximity to shops makes it an extremely useful venue for a social lunch, a travelling stop off, or that revitalising drink whilst shopping. Access and Visa.

LIBERTY Street

LATEST EDITION

THE AMERICAN EATING EXPERIENCE THAT'S BIG NEWS

THE MENU -
A 10 MINUTE THRILLER
Eat Beefsteak Charlie or have a Sweet Sensation, there's Mexican Enchiladas and Chatanooga Chicken. At Liberty Street the food is a true American adventure.

SERVICE AMERICAN STYLE
At Liberty Street we're Big on friendliness, Big on efficiency and Big on hospitality.

THE REAL AMERICAN MEAL
If you thought that American food started and ended with beefburger and fried chicken. Think again!!

COME UP AND SEE US SOMETIME
Liberty Street is open every day from 12 noon until 11pm (10.30pm on Sundays). So come on in for drinks, for snacks, for a meal, for a guaranteed great time.

370 Chorley Road, **Westhoughton,** Bolton BL5 3NB.
Tel: 0942 815900

Alban Retail Park, Winwick Road, **Warrington.**
Tel: 0925 33051

Unit 16, Crown Point Retail Park, **Leeds** LS10.
Tel: 0532 440114

LIBERTY STREET RESTAURANT AND BAR

370 Chorley Road, Westhoughton, Bolton.
Tel: (0942) 815900.
Alban Retail Park, Winwick Road, Warrington.
Tel: (0925) 33051.
Unit 16, Crown Point Retail Park, Leeds.
Tel: (0532) 440114.

Hours:	*12 noon – 11pm (Last orders 10.30pm, 10pm on Sundays).*
Average Prices:	*A la Carte £11.*
Wines:	*A wide variety of wines from £5.95 per bottle.*

For a taste of the real America in the North West, Liberty Street American Restaurants and Bars will appeal to all, regardless of age. Furnished with architectural antiques and genuine all-American 'object d'art', the restaurant will provide interest and entertainment to all drinkers and diners. As a compliment to the decor and style, the menu is a feast for lovers of true American and Mexican food. It is extensive, with something to suit every taste. There are fresh salads, vegetarian specials, steaks, fish dishes and an excellent children's menu. Appetisers of Liberty Street Prawn Catch, Chicken Wingers and Mozzarella Melt can be followed by American delights such as Liberty Street Chicken and Prawns, sizzling Mexican Fajitas, Ribs 'n' Bibs, the inviting Chatanooga Chicken and Ribeye Steak. Some appropriate desserts will conclude — Death by Chocolate, Caribbean Castaway, Mardi Gras or The Three Degrees are a few of the delicacies which suggest themselves.

The extensive wine list combines American newcomers with European favourites — Chardonnay Clos Du, Pinot Noir Firestone and Sinfandel Heitz Vineyard from the USA share the limelight with Cote de Ventous, Sauvignon Blanc and Valpolicella. Enjoy cocktails and mocktails where Shirley Temple meets the Black Russian and Minnehaha basks in the Tequila Sunrise.

Liberty Street Restaurants are large and, with excellent cuisine and vibrant decor, they make attractive venues for any occasion. The restaurant holds speciality and promotional evenings, such as Independence Day and Christmas American-style. Payment by credit card is accepted, whilst those with disabilities will have no problems.

> *It is not our intention to compete with the established 'gourmet guides'. We aim to set the scene and let you, the reader, make the choice. However, we are always pleased to hear from both readers and advertisers, be it praise, recommendations or criticism.*

BASS NORTH

Innkeepers Fayre offers traditional home-cooked pub food such as steak and kidney pie, fish, steaks, a selection of salads and sandwiches, plus daily specials, with an emphasis on quality and value for money.

Staff will be happy to serve half portions to children, or they can select from their own special menu.

You can sample the Innkeepers Fayre at:-

The Gamecock, Whalley Road, Great Harwood, Blackburn,
Tel: 0254 883719.

The Pavilion, Chorley Road, Blackrod, Bolton,
Tel: 0257 474044.

Corks Café Bar, 21/23 Bradshawgate, Bolton.
Tel: 0204 22510
A stylish café bar serving
excellent food in elegant surroundings.

Café Royale, Abergele Road, Colwyn Bay.
Tel: 0492 532180
Home cooked food and morning goods — stop
off whilst sightseeing.

Nabgate, 1 Arthur Road, Harwood, Bolton.
Tel: 0204 24034
A friendly pizza and pasta outlet — opens Easter 1990.

BASS NORTH

THE CHEQUERED FLAG

Parkside Lane, Nateby, Garstang.
Tel: 09952 3071

Located just outside Garstang towards Fleetwood, the Chequered Flag is easily reached from the A6 or M6 motorway.

The 50 seat restaurant offers good value, imaginatively prepared and including several dishes with a continental influence. Steaks in a variety of sauces are popular whilst there are also daily blackboard specials and bar meals. Sunday lunch offers a choice of traditional roast and other main courses with starter/sweet options. A special children's menu is served.

The new conservatory and verandah are popular and the Chequered Flag's vault is a splendid "locals" rendezvous.

THE COCKBECK TAVERN

58 Town Green, Aughtorn, Ormskirk.
Tel: 0695 422889

Located on the Liverpool Road, just out of the centre of Ormskirk, the Cockbeck Tavern was built some one hundred years ago to provide inn fayre and hospitality for local railway workers.

A lounge bar — retaining the original stained glass — was added in the 1970's and the latest improvement to a delightful 40 seat conservatory restaurant.

A good range of food is available lunchtimes and evenings, with the steak grills especially popular. A traditional roast is served in addition to the usual menu at Sunday lunchtime. Children are welcome at lunchtime and early evening.

THE WHITE CROSS

Quarry Road, White Cross, Lancaster.
Tel: 0524 841048

This imaginatively designed hostelry is in an attractive canalside location, close to the centre of Lancaster.

The original building dates back around one hundred and twenty years. It was opened as the White Cross in May 1987 and was awarded a Lancaster Civic Society Commendation for building design.

Food is served in the attractive conservatory restaurant, where the menu is both interesting and excellent value for money. Dishes include stuffed mushrooms, peppered steak and a daily blackboard of specials. Vegetarian dishes are always available and the White Cross is known for 'healthy eating'.

GEORGIAN HOUSE HOTEL

Manchester Road, Blackrod, Bolton. Tel: (0942) 814598.

Hours: *Open for lunch and dinner.*

A meal at the Georgian House Hotel is a memorable occasion. Its Regency Restaurant has one of the best reputations in the North West, a place where not only quality cuisine can be savoured, but also a pleasant atmosphere. Its aura of comfort, courtesy and warmth makes it the choice of discerning diners throughout the week, particularly on Fridays and Saturdays, when the regular dinner dances offer a superb à la carte menu. Changed four times a year with the season, it uses only the best and freshest produce available. Likewise, the daily changing table d'hôte uses only fresh produce. Setting high standards in everything it does, the Georgian House lives up to the greatest expectations, and, as well as a luxurious restaurant, it has 47 de luxe bedrooms, three conference/banqueting suites and a Health and Leisure Club. Situated just one mile from exit six of the M61, it is ideally placed in every way to meet the requirements of the most demanding of guests.

GEORGIAN
HOUSE
HOTEL

Manchester Rd
Blackrod
Bolton
Tel: (0942) 814598

THE MANDERLAY HOTEL AND RESTAURANT

Moses Gate, Farnworth. Tel: (0204) 73661.

Hours:	*Open for lunch and dinner until 10.30pm.*
Average Prices:	*Meals from £3.50.*
Wines:	*House wine from £5.65 per bottle.*

This stylish quasi Italian restaurant has found a successful niche in the 1920's era. Its very name is evocative of the period and is the quintessence of 20's elegance. Walls adorned with prints depicting the 1920's vie for attention with the mahogany and brass fittings, the whole enveloped by Austrian curtains, and a blue and pink colour scheme; lighting imported from Italy completes the ambience. Waitresses dressed in period costume serve an extensive variety of English and Italian cuisine, and the resulting combination of Italy and 1920's England is intriguing, but very engaging. Dine on pastas, spaghetti carbonara, fish dishes such as salmone alla Manderlay, and scampi alla certosina. Sweets are sumptuous, and will leave you wanting more — an Italian style trifle, kiwi fruits in lime sauce, melon balls in crême de menthe. Children's portions and separate menus will ease family dining, and facilities for the disabled are thoughtfully provided. Payment by credit card is accepted.

THE

ℳANDERLAY HOTEL
AND RESTAURANT

13 – 15 BOLTON GATE
MOSES GATE, FARNWORTH

Telephone
(0204) 73661

LAL QUILLA RESTAURANT

Ashton-in-Makerfield, Lancs. Tel: (0942) 271410.

Hours: *Open Mon – Thurs 5.30pm – 12 (midnight); Fri – Sat 5.30pm – 1am; Sunday 1pm – 12 (midnight); Sunday lunch 1pm – 5.30pm.*

Average Prices: *A la Carte £10; Indian cuisine banquet £10.50.*

Enjoy a taste of Indian cuisine in this elegant restaurant. It has a genuine 18th century bar, and regency decor with mahogany furnishings throughout. Surroundings are intimate; candlelit tables are laden with the finest of Indian cuisine — chicken makhani, lamb passanda, or meat dupiaza etc. A monthly ten course banquet is a must for lovers of Indian cuisine.

HONEYSUCKLE INN WITH FORMBY'S

Pool Street, Poolstock, Wigan, Lancs. Tel: (0942) 820079/41551.

Hours: *Open for lunch, dinner (last orders 10.30pm), and bar meals.*

Average Prices: *A la Carte £7; Sun lunch £4.*

Originally built in 1576, The Honeysuckle Inn has recently been rebuilt as part of the Wigan Pier Complex. Dine there on traditional dishes, or upstairs at the Formby's Restaurant, a place frequented by George Formby Jnr and Snr. It features an original Formby signed ukelele, with which guests can have their photo taken. Both à la carte and table d'hôte are available, as well as bar snacks.

WIN A GOURMET DINNER FOR TWO
AT A TOP LOCAL RESTAURANT
VOTE FOR THE

Where to Eat

RESTAURANT OF THE YEAR

We are looking for North West England's Restaurant of the Year, to be featured in the next edition of **Where to Eat.**

During the compilation of the next edition, we shall be asking the region's caterers for their choice of best eating place. However, we would like you, the readers — people who regularly dine out — to take part as well.

A form is provided below for you to tell us what you consider to be the best eating place in the area. It could be an establishment featured in this guide, or a recommendation of your own. And it doesn't matter whether you nominate a formal restaurant, a country inn, a town pub, a wine bar/bistro or even a coffee shop or tearoom.

In addition, the prize of a gourmet meal for two will be awarded to the reader who gives us the best reason for eating out rather than eating in (in not more than 20 words), irrespective of his/her choice of restaurant.

My choice for Restaurant of the Year is

_____

at _____

I prefer to eat out rather than eat in because

_____

_____

Name _____

Address _____

Please send your votes to:
Restaurant of the Year,
Where to Eat in North West England
Kingsclere Publications Ltd.,
2 Highfield Avenue,
Newbury, Berkshire, RG14 5DS

Closing Date: 1 October 1990

Glossary

To assist readers in making the sometimes confusing choice from the menu, we have listed some of the most popular dishes from restaurant featured in *Where to Eat* up and down the country, together with a brief, general explanation of each item. Of course, this can never be a comprehensive listing — regional trends result in variation in the preparation of each dish, and there's no accounting for the flair and versatility of the chef — but we hope it offers readers a useful guideline to those enigmatic menu items.

STARTERS

Foie gras . . . . duck or goose liver, often made into pâté
Gazpacho . . . . a chilled Spanish soup of onion, tomato, pepper and cucumber
Gravad lax . . . . raw salmon marinated in dill, pepper, salt and sugar
Guacamole . . . . a creamy paste of avocado flavoured with coriander and garlic
Hummus . . . . . a tangy paste of crushed chick peas flavoured with garlic and lemon
Meze . . . . a variety of spiced Greek hors d'oeuvre
Moules marinière . . . . mussels in a sauce of white wine and onions
Samosa . . . . small pastry parcels of spiced meat or vegetables
Satay . . . . . . small skewers of grilled meat served with a spicy peanut dip
Taramasalata . . . . a creamy, pink paste of fish roe
Tzatziki . . . . yoghurt with cucumber and garlic
Vichyssoise . . . . a thick, creamy leek and potato soup, served cold

FISH

Bouillabaisse . . . . chunky fish stew from the south of France

Coquilles St Jacques .... scallops
Lobster Newburg .... with cream, stock and, sometimes, sherry
Lobster thermidor .... served in the shell with a cream and mustard sauce, glazed in the oven
Sole Walewska .... a rich dish of poached fish in a Mornay sauce with lobster
Sole bonne femme .... cooked with stock, dry white wine, parsley and butter
Sole véronique .... poached in a wine sauce with grapes
Trout meunière ...... floured, fried and topped with butter, parsley and lemon

MAIN COURSES

Beef Stroganoff .... strips of fillet steak sautéed and served in a sauce of wine and cream
Beef Wellington .... beef in a pastry crust
Boeuf Bourguignon ...... steak braised in a red wine sauce with onions, bacon and mushrooms
Chateaubriand .... thick slice of very tender fillet steak
Chicken à la King .... pieces of chicken in a creamy sauce
Chicken Kiev .... crumbed breast filled with herb butter, often garlic
Chicken Marengo .... with tomato, white wine and garlic
Chicken Maryland ...... fried and served with bacon, corn fritters and fried banana
Osso buco .... knuckle of veal cooked with white wine, tomato and onion
Pork Normandy .... with cider, cream and calvados
Ris de veau .... calves' sweetbreads
Saltimbocca alla romana ...... veal topped with ham, cooked with sage and white wine

Steak au poivre .... steak in a pepper and wine sauce
Steak bordelaise .... steak in red wine sauce with bone marrow
Steak Diane .... steak in a peppered, creamy sauce
Steak tartare .... raw, minced steak served with egg yolk
Tournedos Rossini ..... fillet steak on a croûton, topped with foie gras and truffles
Wiener Schnitzel .... escalope of veal, breadcrumbed and fried

SAUCES

Aioli .... strong garlic mayonnaise
Anglaise .... thick white sauce of stock mixed with egg yolks, lemon and pepper
Arrabbiata .... tomatoes, garlic and hot peppers
Béarnaise .... thick sauce of egg yolks, vinegar, shallots, white wine and butter
Carbonara .... bacon, egg and Parmesan cheese
Chasseur .... mushrooms, tomatoes, shallots and white wine
Dijonnaise ...... cold sauce of eggs and mustard, similar to mayonnaise
Hollandaise .... egg yolks and clarified butter
Mornay ...... creamy sauce of milk and egg yolks flavoured with Gruyère cheese
Pesto .... basil, marjoram, parsley, garlic, oil and Parmesan cheese
Pizzaiola .... tomatoes, herbs, garlic and pepper
Provençale .... tomato, garlic, onion and white wine
Reform .... pepper and white wine with boiled egg whites, gherkins and mushrooms
Rémoulade .... mayonnaise with mustard, capers, gherkins and herbs, served cold

82

DESSERTS

Banoffi pie .... with toffee and banana
Bavarois .... cold custard with whipped cream and, usually, fruit
Crème brûlée .... caramel-topped, rich vanilla flavoured cream
Crêpes Suzette .... pancakes flavoured with orange or tangerine liqueur
Parfait .... chilled dessert with fresh cream
Pavé .... square shaped light sponge
Pavlova .... meringue-based fruit dessert
Sabayon/zabaglione .... whisked egg yolks, wine and sugar
Syllabub .... whipped cream, wine and sherry
Zuccotto .... a dome of liqueur-soaked sponge filled with fruit and cream
Zuppa inglese .... an Italian trifle

CULINARY TERMS

Coulis .... a thin purée of cooked vegetables or fruit
Croustade .... a case of pastry, bread or baked potato which can be filled
Devilled .... seasoned and spicy, often with mustard or cayenne
Dim-sum .... various Chinese savoury pastries and dumplings
Duxelles .... stuffing of chopped mushrooms and shallots
En croûte .... in a pastry or bread case
Farce .... a delicate stuffing
Feuilleté .... filled slice of puff pastry
Florentine .... containing spinach
Goujons .... thin strips of fish
Julienne .... cut into thin slices
Magret .... a cut from the breast of a duck
Mille-feuille .... thin layers of filled puff pastry
Quenelles .... spiced fish or meat balls
Roulade .... stuffed and rolled
Sauté .... to brown in oil
Tournedos .... small slice of thick fillet

Index

ALPHABETICAL INDEX TO ESTABLISHMENTS

ALPHABETICAL INDEX TO TOWNS AND VILLAGES